A Chicago Native and Artistic Pisces, Yolanda "Yo" Jackson first began writing poetry in 1985 and since then she has written volumes of poems, participated in Spoken Word events, and allowed her poems to be used for weddings, birthday celebrations, invitations, greeting cards, homegoings, and so on.

Her poetry captures the essence of everyday life, situations, circumstances, faith, spirituality, encouragement, motivation and more. She is inspired to write by the universe (i.e. people, family, friends, strangers, feelings, thoughts, etc.).

Outside of poetry, Yolanda works as a Senior Paralegal in a large law firm in downtown Chicago. She volunteers with not-for-profit organizations, schools, church and community organizations.

Poetic Flow
Poetry For Your Soul

Yolanda "Yo" Jackson

AuthorHouse™
1663 Liberty Drive, Suite 200
Bloomington, IN 47403
www.authorhouse.com
Phone: 1-800-839-8640

© 2008 Yolanda "Yo" Jackson. All rights reserved.

No part of this book may be reproduced, stored in a retrieval system, or transmitted by any means without the written permission of the author.

First published by AuthorHouse 5/6/2008

ISBN: 978-1-4343-7887-3 (e)
ISBN: 978-1-4343-7886-6 (sc)

Printed in the United States of America
Bloomington, Indiana

This book is printed on acid-free paper.

This book "Poetic Flow – Poetry For Your Soul" is dedicated to all who have come into my life at some point in time and have inspired me in various ways. Each poem was written because of someone or something, because of an event or incident, because of a feeling or a thought. I thank my Mother (Mona Mingo), my best friend (Sha'Ri Hardwick), my late-grandmother (Verena Julia Jackson) and my entire family and friends. It was because of an incident with my Mother that I wrote "About A Lady", it was because of a spiritual conversation with my best friend (Sha'Ri) that she inspired me and suggested I write a poem about Favor, hence "Walking in Faith and Given Favor", and it was because of a conversation held with my late-grandmother in the wee hours of the morning, just talking about life and unfortunate situations that she told me I should write a poem about "Street People." The list goes on and on, but without my family, my friends, my thoughts, my feelings, incidents and circumstances in life, but most importantly GOD'S gift, I would not be able to do "What I Do." I thank each of you for reading my book and it is my heart-felt hope that you will find peace, love, happiness, laughter and even solutions or overcome obstacles because of something you read or saw or heard that changed your life. And I hope that in some way, my book helped you along your journey.

Keep the Faith, it is your light at the end of every tunnel. To GOD be the GLORY in all that you do and all that you receive.

> Much Love,
> Yolanda "Yo" Jackson

Website: www.yolandajackson.bravehost.com
Email: poeticflowyj@yahoo.com

Table of Contents

5 things to keep in mind in your lifetime	1
A Conversation with GOD	2
About A Lady	4
A-Z Black American Poem	5
A Friendship Poem For You	6
All Night	7
It Doesn't Discriminate	8
Deep Thoughts	10
1 night stand	12
What If?	13
Grandmother	14
Street People	15
4-Legged Friend	16
Metamorphosis	17
Mind Over Matter	18
Society v. Reality	20
Quick Lesson About Life	22
The People of Our Nation	23
This World	24
7 day feelings	25
When I	26
Walking in Faith and Given Favor	27
Get It Together	28
A Mother's Love	30
It's not a game	31
This Thing Called Life	34
80's Babies	35
A Friend	36
Our Love	37

Another Year – Another Thanksgiving	38
Black	39
The Trials and Tribulations of Life	40
The creation of a friend	41
Poetic Flow	42
Mean Machine	43
Think About It	44
Stop Trippin - Don't Hate	45
Just Trust	48
Seems Funny	50
A Talk With A Friend	51
When I Look In Your Eyes	52
In The End	53
Looking Back	54
Simple Click	56
Time kept on slippin	57
Poetry in Motion	58
Poetic Reality	60
Have You Ever?	61
Listen Up!	62
Choices	63
Reflections	64
Excuse Me Ms. / Pardon Me Mr.	66
Tick-Tock	68
Don't Block Your Blessings	69
A Love Lost	70
Life In The Fast Lane	71
Neighborhood Drug Dealer	72
Haters	74

The Man at the Entrance	76
Life is too Short	78
Life is like a deck of cards	79
Summertime	80
Little Brother	82
Little Sister	84
God is in my head	86
#1 Consumer	88
My Mind Struggles	90
Hip-hop Memory Lane	92
The Sky Is The Limit	95
What I Do	96
Back In The Day	98
Daily Prayer	101
The Cries of the Street	102
Many paid the price	104
Eyes to the Soul	108
Visions Of The Senses	109
Stars	110
The Stain of Pain	112
A Paradise	115
Weekday Journey	117
Ego Trippin	119
FYI	121
How I feel about you	123
Your Season	125

5 things to keep in mind in your lifetime

Live Life – It's a wonderful gift from GOD
Love Yourself – Because it allows you to love others
Treat Others Kind – Because the blessings you put out, always come back
Smile – Life is too short not too
Pray – It's the most powerful reward

A Conversation with GOD

One day I wondered, why am I here?
What is my purpose?
What is my plan?

I got down on my knees, and asked GOD the same,
First going to him in Jesus Name,
I said "Father GOD, I just don't know, I just don't understand
Why in this life, I was dealt this hand.

Why is my life such a struggle,
Why so much pain,
Oh Father GOD,
I just don't understand."

As I begin to rise from my knees,
I heard a whisper, I felt a light breeze,
A voice begin to speak, such a commanding tone,
I fell back down, with a shiver to my bones.

The voice proceeded to speak and this is what it said,
"Hello my child, your prayer I heard,
So I thought I would tell you in my own words,
I have a plan for your life, that you just can't see,
But continue to do what you do, continue to have faith in me.

I will not steer you wrong, for your path is so bright,
You seem happy during the day, but weary at night,
Fret not my child, for I am your Father above,
I will only show you, Unconditional Love.

You will go through some struggles, you will have some pains
But the rewards you will reap, will be well worth the gain
You have no idea of my plan for you
But you have a purpose in everything you do.

I will not reveal, my plan for your life
But you will see, when the time is right
So don't give up and don't despair
For I am GOD, and are with you everywhere.

I thank you for your prayer,
I enjoyed this conversation and I hope you did too,
Hold tight my child,
Your blessing is about to come through."

About A Lady

Let me tell you about a Lady, who raised 4 babies;
One girl, three boys – all, her pride and joy;
Although there was an age difference between the children;
I have to tell you about this woman.

She went to school and earned her degree;
Encouraged her children to be the best they can be;
She provided clothing, housing and love;
In their eyes, she is a wonderful Mother.

A lady who can stretch a dollar to last more than a week;
Her children, never starving always having something to eat;
She put them first, even before herself;
Working so hard, getting little rest.

Then one day into the hospital she goes;
Fighting for her life and she doesn't even know;
The machines are hooked up, beeping sounds throughout the room;
Many people came & prayed, many faces of gloom.

Then GOD changed the scene, and let me say;
Oh it was a Great Thanksgiving Day!;
God said "Mother, it is time for you to awake;
Your family needs you, so I did not take,
You away from them, but gave you back;
And surely I hope they appreciate that."

That lady, that woman, that mother is none other than my own;
And GOD, I thank you for giving me back my #1;
Mom, I love you and my love stretches to no end;
And I am most grateful to have you as my mother and my very best friend.

A-Z Black American Poem

A is for Achievement of all we've obtained;
B is for Blacks who use their brains;
C is for Courageousness that shows we are brave;
D is for Determination that got us out of being slaves;
E is for Excellence, which we all should achieve;
F is for Freedom, which we all want to see;
G is for Genius, which we all want to be;
H is for Hero's whose wills were to free;
I is for Intelligence, which makes us bold;
J is for Justice so our stories can be told;
K is for Kindness with a heart of gold;
L is for Liberty, which our souls want to hold;
M is for Morality so that we bring no shame;
N is for Non-Violence so that we bring no pain;
O is for Originality the basis of our gain;
P is for Prestigiousness from where we all came;
Q is for Quality the kind of work we do;
R is for Religion so that GOD's light shines down on me & you;
S is for Slavery our ancestors only knew;
T is for Togetherness that got them all through;
U is for Unity, which we need now;
V is for Victory, which means YES! We know how;
W is for Willingness to do what needs to be done;
X is for Xylophones, which were created by the Africans;
Y is for Yesterday, which we should keep in our minds;
Z is for Zulu the greatest warrior of all times.

A Friendship Poem For You

In life many people cross our paths
Some we wish would never had
Some we are ever so glad
Some that always makes us laugh

As we travel through life day after day
We see faces
We see personalities
We see love, hate, spitefulness, envy

Sometimes we wonder what is our purpose?
Why are we here?
What is our job in this world?
Where are we going in life?

And then one day you meet someone
Someone who you connect with
You laugh and talk with
You share things in your life with

One day you meet a Friend
Who keeps a smile on your face
A smile in your heart
And is never too far away
And you don't drift too far apart

A friend, is what I found in you
You can make me smile, when I feel blue
You can pick me up when I'm feeling down
And you are always there, when I need you around

I'm glad we got the chance to meet
You are very kind, ever so sweet
In my heart, you will always have a place
And I thank you, for each step of the way.

All Night

I walked in the house, to the smell of cologne
Knew my man was definitely home
Went into the bedroom, where I found him standing
Walked over to him, and loved the feel of where my hands landed

Strong, sexy, beautiful guy
Makes my knees buckle just thinking, MY oh MY
His lips so smooth, tongue just right
Ready for his loving on this night

His arms so strong, eyes so deep
Looking so erotic, this man I will keep
His touch so soft, he knows what to do
Always telling me "Baby I love you"

His heart so clean, mind so sharp
His figure, like a priceless piece of art
Everything about him, keeps me wanting more
He's so sexy, I just can't help but to adore

He loves me the right way
Always knowing what to say
This man is everything that's right
He can last all night

His stamina so great
And I am his bate
His hands all over me
Mmm, this is how it should be

He keeps me happy and loves me good
Treats me like a real man should
His chest so hard, pecks so tight
I enjoy his loving all day and All Night!

It Doesn't Discriminate

Doesn't matter what you say
Doesn't matter what you do
It doesn't discriminate
Not even against you

Keep playing games
Living life in the fast lane
You've been warned – better take heed
Don't think it's a lie, you better believe

It's all on the radio
You see it on TV
Don't keep down this path
I'm telling you, listen to me

It's an epidemic
All over the world
Taking out races
Men, women, boys and girls

Your skin color/sexuality doesn't matter
It doesn't care
It'll get you whenever, wherever
It is everywhere

It doesn't care that you think you are tough
You think you are hard
This thing right here
Will trip you up and down you'll fall

There's no cure
Just life-prolonging meds
I'm telling you
It took out Charlie, Lynette and Ted

So many ways to get infected
I'm telling you, THINK, don't hesitate
HIV/AIDS
It doesn't discriminate!

I don't personally know of anyone who has contracted HIV/AIDS, but I hope that anyone reading this knows the importance of being extra careful and understands that this disease is deadly, it kills, it does not discriminate.

Deep Thoughts

As I sit here thinking
My eyes blinking
My mind wondering
My heart pondering

Deep thoughts running through my mind
Time after time
Like, why are we at war
With a country next door

Why is there so much hate
Why can't we just appreciate
What we have, who we are
Why are things taken so far

Deep thoughts running through my mind
Time after time
Like, racism is still in existence
People so persistent

Not liking the color of ones skin
Not looking at the person within
Hating on each other
White and black, sister and brother

Deep thoughts running through my mind
Time after time
Like, why is there so much poverty
Why can't there be more prosperity

There is enough money to go around
Why not build housing for homeless from the ground
Put them in a place and help them get back on their feet
So much resistance, no one wants to be defeated

Children are dying each and everyday
This just doesn't seem to be the way
We are suppose to live on this earth
Oh, how it makes my heart hurt

Deep thoughts running through my mind
Time after time
Let's get it together, man, woman, girl and boy
Its time for Life, Laughter and Love

1 night stand

I saw him from across the room,
Physic so fine, Lips divine,
I'm gonna make him mine.

He's walking over,
Look at that brotha,
Sexy eyes, smooth skin,
Oh I know I'm gonna give in.

He says "hey baby, what's your name?
I saw you from over there,
And couldn't help your sexy stare,
So I walked over to catch a glare."

I said "my name is De-Jean,
Brotha you got it going on,
Don't mean to be so blunt,
But I like what I see and what I see I want."

He said "my name is Taylor,
And I'll gladly do you a favor,
Of giving you my all,
At your every beckon call."

And so off we went, to do our thang,
Holding steadfast to those fake ass names,
But it was all worth the ride of such a sexy man,
And that's the story of my 1 Night Stand.

What If?

What if the sky wasn't blue?
What would everyone do?
What if the clouds were not white?
Would the world be right?

What if there were no oceans & seas?
Where would this earth be?
What if everyone was the same?
Whenever we did something wrong, who would we have to blame?

What if there was no sun or moon?
Would this earth had been made so soon?
What if there was no Love?
What would we think of the man above?

What if we had no peace?
Would the emerging of chaos ever cease?
What if dogs and cats could always get along?
Would this earth be a place where a chaos of people belonged?

What if earth was never thought of?
Would we be in the Heavens above?

Grandmother

You were good, you were great
When I was feeling down you gave me faith

Just like my mother, you taught me right from wrong
When I was a baby falling asleep, you'd sing me a song

When I needed you, you were always there
With open arms, full of love and care

Grandmother, you meant the world to me
I'm the luckiest grand-daughter there could ever be

But now you are gone, to the heavens in the sky
I try my best to not cry

I know you are happier, healthier than you've ever been
But when you were called home, I lost my best friend
I'll always love you and remember all you shared,
You opened my heart and taught me how to really care

You were the only person who gave me unconditional love,
I know you are smiling down on me from the heavens above

I thank you for sharing your life, love, and molding me to be the best I can be,
Grandmother, I look forward to seeing you again, so hold a place for me.

For my grandmother (Verena Julia Jackson 1933-1994)

Street People

We are the people of the streets – We have nothing to eat.

I asked you for money to get some bread – But you
    looked at me and nothing was said.

You live in fancy houses up on the hills – While I
    live down here praying for a meal.

You walk the streets up and down – Passing me by with an irritable frown.
I asked if you had any food or money to spare
    – You ignored me as if I wasn't there.
You zoom past in your fancy cars – Passing me by, going so far.

All I have to keep me warm are my blankets, boxes and sheets
    – Hoping and praying that I'll soon get something to eat.

All I asked for was a dime – You looked at me as if I had committed a crime.

The children are dying from starvation of food – And when I
    asked if you had anything to spare, you acted so rude.

What if it were you on the streets? – What if you had nothing to eat?

You act as if us street people don't exist – And when we ask
    you for a little something, you always resist.

Even though I live on the streets and you treat me odd – You must always
    remember that we were created equally by the **Almighty GOD.**

    Inspired to write by my late grand-mother (Verena Julia Jackson)

4-Legged Friend

I remember when you were small
Now you're getting so tall
You follow me around
Acting like a little clown
Keeping me laughing
All daylong
Even when you do something you know is wrong

I've learned from you
You have learned from me
Together we are
Fancy free

You make sure I'm okay
Sending me off each day
With a waddle of your tail
A scratch on my arm from your nail

When I come home, you greet me at the door
Smelling my clothes, wondering where I've been
Waiting to go outside
To play with your friends

You brighten my days
And ease my nights
So loveable and cute
So playful, so right

My little buddy
My 4-legged friend
I could take you and raise you
All over again

You've got your own personality
And some of mine too
You are a joy to have
And I'm glad I have you

Metamorphosis

From the Sperm to the Egg -
To the wait in a dark place -
To the food through the Mother -
To the birth.

From the crawl to the walk -
The laughter to the talk -
The good to the bad -
The happy to the sad.

To the highest of the high -
From the lowest of the low -
Wondering where did -
Your great life go.

It started out -
From the streets to the house -
To drinking fancy drinks -
Paying for things, not worried about the cost.

From no shoes to many -
Unemployment to an Empire -
From rags to riches -
And all you desired.

From the lavish clothes -
To the house on the hill -
Loosing it all -
To the man who sold you the illegal pills.

From the kids to the wife -
The fancy job -
Making big paper -
Then came the fall.

You sit back thinking -
How your experience in life was -
And then how it is -
Life simply put, is a metamorphosis.

Over Mind Matter

MIND OVER MATTER IS WHAT THEY SAY
IF YOU THINK IT, IT'LL BE THAT WAY
IF YOU DON'T MIND, THEN IT DOESN'T MATTER
IF IT DOESN'T MATTER, THEN YOU DON'T MIND
PLAYING WITH YOUR HEAD, TIME AFTER TIME

WHAT ARE YOU TALKING ABOUT, THAT'S NOT REAL
WHO SAID THAT WAS THE DEAL
WHEN DID THAT HAPPEN
WHERE AND WHEN
IT'S NOT REAL, ONLY PRETEND
IF YOU DON'T MIND, THEN IT DOESN'T MATTER
IF IT DOESN'T MATTER, THEN YOU DON'T MIND
PLAYING WITH YOUR HEAD, TIME AFTER TIME

YOU WOKE UP THIS MORNING IN A STRANGE PLACE
LOOKED RIGHT INTO THE EYES OF AN UNKNOWING FACE
WONDERING HOW YOU GOT THERE IN THE FIRST PLACE
TRYING TO FIGURE OUT, NOW YOU HESITATE
TO ASK SOME QUESTIONS YOU REALLY NEED TO KNOW
THINK ABOUT IT, GRAB YOUR STUFF AND GO
IF YOU DON'T MIND, THEN IT DOESN'T MATTER
IF IT DOESN'T MATTER, THEN YOU DON'T MIND
PLAYING WITH YOUR HEAD, TIME AFTER TIME

THINKING ABOUT BIG THINGS
MAKING PLANS, HAVING BIG DREAMS
EXPLORING THE WORLD, PLACE BY PLACE
LEARNING HOW TO REALLY NEGOTIATE
GOT IT FIGURED OUT EXACTLY WHAT TO DO
LOOKING IN THE MIRROR, NOT REALLY SEEING YOU
IF YOU DON'T MIND, THEN IT DOESN'T MATTER
IF IT DOESN'T MATTER, THEN YOU DON'T MIND
PLAYING WITH YOUR HEAD, TIME AFTER TIME

FINALLY LAYING DOWN AT THE END OF THE DAY
YOUR MIND TRAVELING ON ITS OWN WAY
THE SUN HAS WENT DOWN – NOW IT IS NIGHT
THOUGHTS STRUGGLING ABOUT THE DAY, HAVING ITS OWN FIGHT
THINKING AND THINKING TRYING TO FIGURE OUT
WHAT THIS LIFE IS ALL ABOUT
IF YOU DON'T MIND, THEN IT DOESN'T MATTER
IF IT DOESN'T MATTER, THEN YOU DON'T MIND
PLAYING WITH YOUR HEAD, TIME AFTER TIME

Society v. Reality

Society says, "This is how it must be"
Reality says, "Yeah we'll see"

Society says, "You must do it this way"
Reality says, "You will do what I say"

Society says, "You have no other choice"
Reality says, "You do have a voice"

Society says, "How dare you say that!"
Reality says, "There's no need to step back"

Society says, "Oh no, that is wrong"
Reality says, "Do what you do, on your own"

Society says, "You are making a mistake"
Reality says, "Keep it real, don't be a fake"

Society says, "Two wrongs don't make a right"
Reality says, "Kick ass, it's going to be a fight"

Society says, "Let the proper authorities take care of it"
Reality says, "Its do or die, SHIT"

Society says, "All in do time"
Reality says, "I have to take what's mine"

Society says, "It'll take its course, just let it go"
Reality says, "Oh, HELL NO!"

Society v Reality it's a tug-of-war
Stuck between two places not wanting to handle any more
Pick your battles along with your fights
Day by day and Night by night
Which is correct? What do I do?
It's just too much, which do I choose?
Society says NO, but Reality says YES
Is this a game? Is this a test?
I have to choose, but which should it be
Society or Reality, Hell I give up, I just choose me
Whichever decision I make, whether it be either / or
Fact of the matter is I just can't take it anymore
Too many decisions, too many thoughts
The choice is mine and I have to live with my faults
Since the choice is only between these too,
It's about me and yours is about you.
Society v Reality, the confusion it can bring
Just keep your focus, keep your faith, it'll get you through anything.

Quick Lesson About Life

Life is a big ball of experiences.

In order for you to experience it,

You must live life.

In order to live your life,

You must love life.

In order to love life,

You must love thyself.

Once this is done,

Your possibilities are limitless.

The People of Our Nation

The people of our nation have no realization.
They cheat, steal, and lie;
Thinking that's going to get them by;
They don't realize we are the future and our parents are the past;
But most young people are moving along too fast.

The people of our nation have no realization.
They're tooting, drunk and high on drugs;
Hanging out with all the thugs;
They've dropped out or gotten kicked out of school and have no education;
Not realizing education is the key to succession.

The people of our nation have no realization.
The young, old, poor and rich;
All their doing is digging their grave ditch;
Hanging out and being on the streets means nothing at all;
Because the bigger you are the harder you fall.

The people of our nation have no realization.
The junkies, drug dealers, and pushers you see;
May never have strived to the best of their abilities;
Instead of rising to the glistening lights of the heavens bells;
They fell all the way down into the slums of hell;
GOD created man, woman, oceans, seas, animals, and plants;
He didn't create cocaine, pcp, angel dust, and crack.

The people of our nation have no realization.
Drugs mess up your mind;
You lose track of time;
So to the people of our nation, take these words from me;
DON'T FALL DOWN, RISE UP IN SOCIETY!

This World

This World,
Is full of twists, turns, and twirls
This World,
Can be a piercing of a glowing pearl
This World,
Is more peaceful in the heavens above
This World,
Is full of ups and downs
This World,
Is being twirled all around
This World,
Is full of good and bad / happy and sad
This World,
Was made for you and me
And we must make it out to be the best it can be

7 day feelings

Sunday – praise

Monday – blues

Tuesday – woo's

Wednesday – tired

Thursday – glad

Friday – thrills

Saturday – chill

When I

WHEN I CAN'T SEE WITH THE NAKED EYE,
A MICROSCOPE CAN SEE IT FINE.

WHEN I CAN'T DO ANYTHING WITH MY HANDS,
A DEVICE CAN HELP ME CREATED BY MAN.

WHEN I CAN'T WALK WITH MY FEET,
I SIT IN A WHEELCHAIR SEAT.

WHEN I CAN'T HEAR,
I USE A GADGET TO PUT IN MY EAR.

WHEN I CAN'T MOVE MY NECK,
I USE A BRACE SO IT CAN REST.

WHEN I CAN'T DO ANYTHING AT ALL,
I FEEL LIKE A NEWBORN BABY WHO
    HASN'T YET LEARNED TO CRAWL.

WHEN I CAN DO ALL THESE THINGS
    AND BE THE BEST I CAN BE,
I FEEL LIKE AN INNOCENT PERSON WHO
    HAS BEEN LOCKED UP FOR MANY
    YEARS AND IS NOW FINALLY FREE.

Walking in Faith and Given Favor

With all that's going on in the world today; Have you
    ever wondered, what could you say?
To help yourself understand; The power of the Almighty Hand.

Does your mind ever wonder? Your brain ever think?
Of the Lord above; Being the strongest Link.

They have taken GOD out of the school; And we
    wonder why children act a fool
The sheer presence and mention of his name; Is such a glorious gain.

Have you ever thought about your life? Wondered if
    you're doing something wrong or right?
Struggling with demons deep within; Wanting the chaos within you to end.

Looking over your life and where you have been; To the place you are now
Sitting back just mesmerized; Stunned, and thinking HOW?

Being in situations; You just didn't know how to handle
Felt like you were riding high waves; In a tiny boat, without a paddle

Sometimes not understanding how you made it through;
When you knew with absolute certainty;
That the one who was blessed, surely should not have been you.

Glancing at your surroundings; And trying to figure out
The circle that surrounds you; And what's its all about.

Day after day, you got better and better;
    Continuously kneeling down in Prayer
And GOD saw and he surely knew; You were
    walking in Faith and gave you Favor.

And now you understand; The power of the Almighty Hand
The gloriousness of the Father Above; Continuously
    giving unconditional love.

Faith and Favor; Favor and Faith
What an awesome pair; Thank you Heavenly Father for always being there.

Get It Together

When you said it was over –
I didn't know what to do –
I cried and cried everyday –
Tears of pain over you.

I gave so much –
I got so little –
My heart was broken –
Oh I felt so pitiful.

I loved you dearly –
With all of my heart –
I just wanted to be with you –
Never wanted to be apart.

I cried until my eyes were dry –
There was nothing left for any tears –
All my time and love –
Wrapped up in so many years.

Until one day I realized –
I think I'm better today –
I've done all my crying –
I'm looking the other way.

I always thought –
It would be me and you forever –
Until I finally realized –
I just need to get it together.

You didn't make me –
But this is what I believed –
Thought I couldn't live without you –
Huh, Boy please.

Yeah you had me going –
But only for a short while –
Glad I didn't wallow to long –
But then again, that's not my style.

I'm moving on –
Headed in a different direction –
Living my life to the fullest –
Without any hesitation.

Thank you for letting me go –
It was really for the better –
Cause now I'm doing my thing –
Oh yeah, I definitely got it together!

A Mother's Love

A Mother's Love;
Like the Heavens above.
She cradles you tight;
Throughout the night.
She watches you grow;
Never wanting to let go.
She holds your hand Tight, lovingly, grand;
She tells you things to help you learn;
To use in life later on.
She has hopes and dreams;
Of you achieving great things.
She bore you 9 months with grace;
Making sure to never lose pace.
She agonized the pain;
She fed your brain.
She released you into this world;
Oh what a beautiful baby boy, baby girl.
She loved you inside and out;
You are her child, there is no doubt.
She believes in you before you are here;
She rejoices with happy tears.
She disciplines you to make you strong;
She corrects you every time you are wrong.
She agrees with you when you are right;
She holds you when she hugs you with all her might.
She assures you that it'll all be okay;
She kisses you and awaits the next day.
She fusses at you when you've made her mad;
She smiles at you when you've made her glad.
A Mother's Love is an Eternal Inspiration;
She gives you your ultimate Motivation.
A Mother's Love will always be true;
Your Mother's Love is forever instilled in YOU.

It's not a game

Woke up this morning
Started on your way
Hoping that you will have
A safe and prosperous day

Gunshots unloading
Throughout the night
Wondering if a bullet
Will put out your light

A lady walks to the door
To pick up the mail
A bullet takes her life
What a sad story to tell

Walking out of the store
Getting in your car
A gun in your back
What kind of shit is that?

Sitting in your house
Get up to get some water
Gunfire rings out
Bullet through your window, hitting your daughter

(continues)

Friends out having fun
Shopping for the holiday season
Get robbed by a masked man with a gun
What is the REASON?

It's not a game
People are disturbed
Stealing, Killing, Hurting
It just angers my soul

6-year old child
Playing at the school
Car speeds down the street, jumps the curb
Driving like a fool
The car hits the boy
DAMN! It's too late
Shit just ain't right
How much more can we take?

Doctor misdiagnosed the patient he had
Turns out medication that was taken
Was way too bad
Loved one gone, and who's to blame
Medical malpractice – It's not a game

Walking down the street
Feeling good and plenty
Car drives up, window comes down
Ah SHIT! – Mistaken identity

This world is crazy
What do we do?
It's not a game
But it involves me and you

Walk into the job, getting ready to work
Get called into the office
Now you are being wrote up
For some bull-shit lie that someone told
Watch over your shoulder, people are COLD

There's no love lost between two friends
One sets the other up
Now a life has come to an end

Mom always said, everyone that's good to you is not good for you
But you never want to listen
Now the people you thought had your back
Are the same one's who are snitching

You are locked up, while your so-called friend is out
See that's the shit, mom was talking about
Don't put all your ducks in one row
Because you'll be the first duck to go

Open your eyes
Pay attention
It's not a game
When will you listen?

Stop thinking you know everything about life
Especially when you are doing wrong, instead of right
Stop, just stop placing blame!
You need to recognize, it's not a game

This Thing Called Life

When nothing seems to go your way;
When all things seem to be astray;
When beauty doesn't seem to come in the month of May
That's life, what can one say?

As you strive to be the best;
Obstacles put you to the test;
You wonder – What is this mess?
Just pray and let GOD do the rest.

When plans backfire in your face;
And you feel you're in a never-ending race;
When things are not going at a steady pace;
Try to keep your head high and walk with grace.

As the hours, days, and months go by;
You find yourself laughing, so you don't cry;
When your family doesn't seem to care;
And your friends are not there;
When you seem to be standing in the middle of nowhere;
You kneel down in prayer;
Because it's the only way you'll find the answer you're looking for;
To lead you to a brighter day.

Yeah, this thing called Life has its ups and downs;
It's dark at times, but the light ultimately shines through;
And this is when you know, GOD is shining down on you!

80's Babies

Oh no, tell me why!
Our youth continue to die;
With the pull of a trigger or stabbing of a knife;
Young people have no regard for the human life.

Drug dealers, pushers, gang-bangers & young hookers;
Turning on the news, seeing more and more;
This is an issue across racial boards.

So many past struggles, so many lives lost;
And young people don't realize the cost;
From segregation to education;
Slavery, concentration camps and race relations.

What is it going to take, to make them understand;
The worth of the lives of boys, girls, woman and man?
Stop the violence and the genocide;
Wake up and realize;
The value of life and its worth;
From the conception to the birth.

80's babies, what went wrong?
This world needs you to be strong;
Be powerful, positive forces and leave the B.S. alone;
Sit down, pick up a book and learn where you come from.

The advantages that you have, that were not here before;
You can walk through a brand new door.

Show the next generation a positive light;
And do away with the senseless fights;
The killing, stealing – the hurt and the pain;
Give life a chance and start to live again.

80's babies, you are a special kind;
So always keep in mind;
The world is yours, with so much good to do;
It's an open playground and what it's missing is you.

A Friend

A friend is someone you can count on –
You and your friend can always have fun –
A friend can cheer you up when you're feeling down –
You and your friend can always clown around –
A friend is someone you can always trust –
A friend will always help you, no matter what –
A friend is someone you can always talk to –
A friend no matter good or bad will always help you through –
If you have a friend, who doesn't like to help, talk to you or call –
That wasn't your friend to begin with, they were not your friend at all.

Our Love

Is it my hair or is it my eyes;
Maybe it's my fabulous style.
Is it my nose or my lips;
Maybe it's my switch.
Is it my walk or is it my talk;
Maybe it's because of what I'm about.

Do you love my speech or is it my ways;
Maybe its how I make you feel every day.
Do you love my clothes or is it my skin;
Maybe its how I make you feel deep within.
Do you love my fingers or is it my hands;
Maybe its because I stand back and let you be the man.

Is it the house or is it the car;
Maybe its because we can't stand to be apart.
Do you love my arms or is it my legs;
Maybe its because we seem to have it made.
Is it my fire or is it my desire;
Maybe its because we both want to aspire.
Do you love my strength or is it my motivation;
Maybe its because we have made a beautiful creation.

You are my heart, you are my soul;
When you found me, together we found gold;
You said I am your future, your soul mate;
Our love will always conquer any hate;
You are my backbone, You are my life;
You are my husband and I am your wife.

Is it your eyes or is it your arms;
That makes me feel protected in any storm.
Is it your hands or is it your lips;
That makes me feel a chill with every kiss.
Is it your clothes or is it your skin;
That when I see you, I fall in love all over again.

It is both you and also me;
That we belong together and our love was meant to be.

Another Year - Another Thanksgiving

So another year has almost gone;
Wow, how fast each year comes;
Each one with new hopes and dreams;
Aspirations, motivations, so many things;
The one thing that really catches my heart;
Is all my family and friends, whether near or far;
It's that time of year to give thanks for the year that has been;
So I write this to all of my friends;
For those whom I've known for numerous years;
For the ones who we've shared a shoulder full of tears;
For the ones that keep me laughing whenever we speak;
For the ones that I just happened to meet;
For the friends in my life for all sorts of reasons;
Whether it is for a lifetime or if only for a season;
I thank each of you for the times we have shared;
I thank each of you for the burdens we've helped to bear;
For the ones who I haven't known for very long;
For the ones who have kept me very strong;
To my girls and my guys that have been there for me;
To all my friends, who are true to thee;
I thank you for this year, past years and the ones to come;
I look forward to sharing with you, a life full of fun;
To all my friends, old and new;
I thank you for keeping me grounded and always being true;
Each of you has given me something in my life that I'll always hold on to;
I thank you for everything, but most importantly, I thank you for being YOU.

Thank You!!

Black

Black is a color, unlike any other;
Black is my race, black is my face;
Black is you, black is me;
Black is what it was intended to be;
Black is not only the color of a crayon, it is a color deep beyond;
Black is proud, that's why we stand out amongst the crowd;
Black is bold, that's why we have superb stories that are told;
Black is beautiful, that's we steadily move forward and are not stuck in neutral;
Black is all these things and much more created from above;
But most importantly, BLACK IS LOVE

The Trials and Tribulations of Life

I tell you, this world is a trip,
Everyone walking around thinking they are hip.

Ain't nobody going to get nowhere acting like that,
And if you ask me, I say that's a fact.

You can't hardly find a sain person around anymore,
That's because everyone's doing what they want behind closed doors.

You walk down the streets and all you see are junkies, drugs, and hooks,
Hell, you can't hardly find anyone in the library or house reading an
    educated book.

What's wrong with the people? They have nothing to do,
But they know how to point their finger at you.

Movies and rap songs have so much exploitation,
Many young kids growing up now, have no knowledge of true realization.

The mother and or father are doing drugs all the time,
The child raising them self doesn't even have a steady mind.

Huh, I tell you the trials and tribulations of life is a mess,
Keep GOD first, do your best, and let him take care of the rest.

The creation of a friend

When god created me, he brought a new meaning to life again;
For before there was just a lonely person, so through trust and honesty, god created a friend.

God knew I needed a friend to share my kindness or joy I might find;
A friend with a heart that is both strong and good, a heart that would always be kind.

From that date to this, god has placed a friend for me with a wondrous mind and heart of love;
He has given you beauty, honesty, and trust that shines from within and a wisdom from above.

Poetic Flow

This poetic flow that I have
My pen to the paper, damn I'm bad
The words just guide
From my hand to the pad

It's like a thought unfinished
Until my hand and wrist get to itching
Then the words flow out so slick, so smooth
Like my personality, so very cool

It just hits me like a flash of light
Then I begin to write
Rhyming words and phrases
Always giving praises

I don't know how I got it
Where it came from
But I take my pen and paper
And with a thought I run

Writing words as they come to mind
Never hesitating, just writing my rhymes
I don't know how it happens, but one thing I know
God blessed me, with this Poetic Flow

Mean Machine

IS IT THE CEO
THE HEAD OF THE CLASS
THE WHITE COLLAR WORKER
OR THE MAN COLLECTING THE TRASH?

IS IT THE COURTROOM LAWYER
THE ER DOCTOR
THE RESTAURANT WAITER
OR THE VALET PARKER?

IS IT THE GROCERY STORE OWNER
THE CORNER REC
THE PROFESSIONAL SPORTS PLAYER
OR THE BOOKEY TAKING YOUR BET?

IS IT THE ASTRONAUT IN OUTER SPACE
THE PILOT FLYING THE PLANE
THE DEDICATED BUS DRIVER
OR THE CONDUCTOR ON THE TRAIN?

IS IT THE TEACHER
HOW ABOUT THE PROFESSOR
THE NEWS ANCHOR
OR THE METEROLOGIST PREDICTING THE WEATHER?

THE REFLECTION
HIGH AND LOW
EVERYWHERE YOU LOOK
THERE IT GOES.

IT'LL FIND YOU
WHEN YOU REALIZE IT IS NO LONGER A DREAM
ONE DAY YOU'LL LOOK IN THE MIRROR
AND WHAT LOOKS BACK
IS THE MEAN MACHINE.

Think About It

We all have our problems * Some more than others
Many times we take for granted * Our loved ones (husbands, wives, friends,
sisters, brothers, fathers and mothers)

We get caught up in ourselves * Sometimes thinking we are better than some
Truth be told – we may be better at "something" * But we are better than none

Some forget where they come from * When the money starts to stack high
Our noses stare to the sky * Not uttering a word to a passer-by

Why do we act the way we do? * Why must you
not like me and I in return not like you?
Why do we belittle one another without hesitation? *
We are all a part of GOD'S great creation

I love myself and those around * I've been known to make
one smile when they originally wore a frown
We need to uplift, motivate and encourage one another
When opportunity knocks, grab hold of its throat and fight off the odds
For we would not be a people
If there was no GOD

THINK ABOUT IT!

Stop Trippin – Don't Hate

Stop trippin
Don't hate
Because I have a nice job
And I'm getting paid

I have nice clothes
Drive a cool car
Keep my hair and nails done
And live kind of far

Stop trippin
Don't hate
Because I speak in a professional tone
And live in a large home

I have a swimming pool
A Jacuzzi too
Living a beautiful life
And trust me I do

Stop trippin
Don't hate
Because I make big dollars
And just got some nice flowers

I have a huge office overlooking the water
Still getting educated
Getting smarter and smarter
Using my mind to make a change
And you thought I was a bit strange

I remember when we met
And I told you my goals
Told you I was on a mission
Said I had so much ambition

(continues)

Told you I wanted to help so many people
The world needed me in all of its evil
You told me I sound like a real go-getter
But didn't think I could make anything better

You told me I was just wishing
And I may be missing
Something else in life
Why waste my time trying to do so much right

I told you I loved helping others
It gave me a sense of worth
Made me feel good
Like a mother holding her child after giving birth

Now that I've made it
With my name on the wall
Have my own business
I'm standing tall

Doing everything I said
I wanted to do
Now you have the audacity to trip
Shame on you

Stop trippin
Don't hate
This was my blessing
It was my fate

Many times people will doubt you
But you have to keep on your path
Because GOD will deal you a hand
And the equation is much bigger than simple math

So I say to you all
It's never too late

But when the enemy comes
Tell them
Stop trippin
Don't hate!

Just Trust

Today when I woke up
I took a good look around
Looked at my surroundings
Wondering what could be found

Starring in the mirror
With a smile on my face
Thanking the Good Lord
For his Mercy and His Grace

Thinking about the day before
And the day as it was
Its a new beginning for me
Like a new piece of a puzzle

Yesterday is gone
Tomorrow is yet to come
Today is what I have to work with
The weather is so nice, sky so bright with the morning sun

So I walked out of the house
Thanking the Lord for such a beautiful day Thinking
    of all his blessings As I drove along my way
I prayed periodically
While driving in the car
Sometimes my mind just wondered
Ever so far

I thought about my life
My family and my friends
And I thanked the Lord again
For a brand new beginning
I went along my day
Working and talking
Sitting and laughing
Standing and walking

I finished my day
And begin my travel back home
Listening to my music
Snapping my fingers along

I arrived home safely
Got out of the car
Went back into the house
Mind still wondering ever so far

I thanked the Lord for blessing me this day For
    keeping me safe As I traveled along my way

I thanked him for his mercy
I thanked him for his grace
He kept me protected
And kept harm out of my way

If we just trust in him
Like we do in so many other things
I promise you
An abundance of joy like no other, it what he will bring.

Seems Funny

Seems funny how time fly's
Right before your eyes
At one point life starts
Then it stops

Seems funny how times change
Bringing more or less pain
One day you wake up with it all
The next you realize you've taken a fall

Seems funny how people meet
Sometimes while on the street
Other times through school, someone or on the job
Some people seem normal –others seem odd

Seems funny how people relate
Even when they negotiate
A deal's – a deal
Guess they have to "keep it real"

Seems funny how people love
Sometimes giving thanks first to the Father above
Many if not all want it in return
Giving love and not receiving is not a good feeling to some

Seems funny how life is
Sometimes good, other times bad
It has its ups and downs that we must deal with
Sometimes happy, other times sad

Seems funny how things seem funny
The world is a chaotic and hectic place
You have to live one day at a time
Live, laugh, love and enjoy the sunshine

A Talk With A Friend

I had a talk with my friend,
Let me tell you how the talk began.

I said "friend I have something to say,
And I have to tell you today.

My friend, what is wrong with you?
Is there something I can do?

You look like you're falling apart,
All under your eyes are dark.

I hope you're not doing what I think you are,
Because if you are, you're not going to make it far.

Can't you see you are ruining your mind,
After awhile you are going to lose track of time.

If you keep using drugs like candy,
You're going to find yourself more useless than handy.

My friend, can't you see you are causing pain,
Stop using PCP and COCAINE.

You look like you're hooked and strung,
You'll soon find yourself gone.

You are my friend, that's why I'm talking to you,
I'm trying to save you, so please do as I ask you to.

You **must** stop now or else you will find,
We will be **waiting** no more, there will be no more time.

I **hope this** talk with you my friend,
Has made **you realize**, if you don't stop your life will very soon end."

When I Look In Your Eyes

When I look in your eyes,
The beauty I see,
Brings such joy to me.

I remember when you were a baby,
Trying to walk,
Listening to baby noises,
Then hearing you talk.

I think back on your first day at school,
Then your first graduation,
The proud feeling I had,
So much admiration.

You were a joy to be around,
Such a little clown,
But always loving in your ways,
Oh how I remember those days.

Now you are all grown up,
With a family of your own,
Raising your own children,
Living in your own home.

Even still, when I see you to this day,
I look in your eyes, and I still can see,
The beauty of my child,
Staring back at me.

You have brought me so much joy,
Laughter and love over the years,
My beautiful baby,
My eyes filled with tears.

You continue to achieve and overcome all that life brings your way,
Live your life, day by day,
Love yourself and always be true,
When I look in your eyes, I see such a beautiful you.

In The End

I look at myself and those around
Some have smiles and other frown
Things go wrong everyday
But you have to hold your head high in some way
Life is a learning experience and it can be hard
The choice is yours how you play your cards

We all make mistakes at many points in time
We must learn from them – I'm learning from mine
Sometimes we make them over & over again
Life is a learning experience from beginning to end

Don't blame yourself for lifetime mistakes
Because you'll always hold your head down & may lose faith
Just know whatever you did, you tried your best
Besides being a life experience, it's also a test

With all things you do, the goal is to succeed
It's all about what you make it out to be
Never bear the burden of two
Because the burden surrounds the both of you

Never give up on your hopes and dreams
With determination & motivation, one day they'll be
real and maybe closer that what they seem
Always know you have a father above
Who sprinkles down upon you nothing but love

Even when it seems like the problems you have, you won't make it through
Don't be surprised when all burdens are gone
and the heavenly father uplifts you
Keep the faith in he who is above
Within yourself, always have love
Sometimes it seems this is all we have to grab on to
IN THE END – You'll come back a stronger and better you

Looking Back

When I look back and see / All that I use to be / I
    drop down and pray / Each and every day

I thank GOD for his grace and mercy / For all he has done /
    He shaped me and molded me / And now I am one

I fell by the wayside / And everyone I knew forgot
    about me / They tossed me out /
Without giving a second thought

I know I messed things up / I know I did some dirt / I know
    I wasn't right / And I know I did a lot to hurt

I can't take back those times / I can't rewind the clock / I've
    asked for people's forgiveness / But they forgave me not

I hung my head down low / Didn't know what to
    do / I was an outcast / Until I found you

I gave you my heart / My soul and my all / You never turned
    away from me / Even when I continued to fall

You gave me a new life / A breathe of fresh air /
    You restored me and gave me faith /
You reminded me that you were there

Now I walk with my head high / Proud of what I've become /
    Thanking GOD each and every day / For all he has done

I sometimes sit down / And reflect over my life /
    Realizing that the people I loved most /
Gave up on me without a fight

I understand to a certain extent / Because I was no Angel / But
    when I showed I had changed / There was still so much anger

GOD turned my life around / How very humble
    I am for that / Now I can truly say /
I'm moving forward and not looking back!

Sometimes we forget that when we knell down in prayer we ask GOD to forgive us for things we've done and we expect that he will forgive us, because he is a forgiving GOD. But why is it when someone else asks us to forgive them, we just can't seem to do it or either refuse to. What if GOD did you the same way when you prayed to him? Let's not forget that one of GOD's greatest commandments was to LOVE each other. Think about that the next time someone asks for forgiveness from you ☺.

Simple Click

People don't talk everyday
Nor do we see each other everyday
But we will email each other on a daily basis

All kinds of emails float around
Some good, some not so good
Some funny, some just a hot mess
Other emails come along and people are blessed

Anyone can be sitting at the computer
Having such a rough day
YOU'VE GOT MAIL
And they love what their screen displays

People have contemplated suicide
Just waiting for the right time
But a ringtone from the computer
A message sublime

Government has tried to keep him away
Out of the schools, no talking about Christ
But GOD finds a way
To make many wrongs into a right

So the next time you get an inspirational email
When you are feeling down a bit
Share it with others, because you never know
The power of a Simple Click

Time kept on slippin

He said he would go to a new place
Said he wanted to see some new faces
Was tired of the same old thing
Wanted to fulfill some dreams

He saw some things on the television
He was destined on a mission
Kept on hoping and wishing
Figured he would be really persistent

Yeah he was ready for the world
Like giving a nut to a squirrel
So anxious and ready to go
Thought things would move fast, but they begin to move slow

Started hanging out with some guys
His truths became lies
His life at a halt
Not giving much thought

The days went past
The weeks carried on
The months flew by
The years of a young boy scorned

The dreams that were once perpetuated
Of a boy that long ago had no hesitation
To tell the story of his success one day
Seems to have faded away

That's when reality hits
You begin to think about what once was
And realize you were so busy trippin
That time kept on slippin

Poetry in Motion

Poetry in Motion
Just like the Ocean
Waves so high
Just rolling by

Flowing so smooth
Writing too deep
Making minds wonder
Where are the words I keep

The writer keeps writing
Thought after thought
Keeping up with the flow
Not letting it stop

Poetry in Motion
The words are strong
Like a powerful wind
In a winter storm

Keeping readers on edge
Taking the book to bed
Reading what's said
Feeling the flow from foot to head

This ride is great
The flow so smooth
Never missing a beat
Always keeping my cool

Poetry in Motion
Like a summer day
A light breeze on your face
As you travel on your way

The power of the mind
The letters coming together
Writing it all down
Just doesn't get any better

Releasing thoughts
Time after Time
Poetry in Motion
Rhyme after Rhyme

Poetic Reality

Putting words into verses
Verses into rhymes
Getting into your minds
Each and every time

The reality of the world
The news we all see
Knowing at any moment
It could be you or me

Listening to people talk
About all kinds of things
Hearing good stories and bad ones
And some funny ones in between

Being frustrated about situations
Wondering what's going to happen next
Not understanding some outcomes
Some things leaving you perplexed

So with words I express
The stories I hear
Some from far away
Some very close and dear

Thoughts running in my head
Words scrambling in my mind
Searching for the next title
Looking for the next sign

Getting stumped
Writers block
Trying to keep it going
Trying to stay on top

Okay, okay I got it now
Life is a poem – as well as society
So I present to you my new book
Poetic Reality

Have You Ever?

Have you ever went to sleep; Had a dream;
Woke up; And thought about some things?

Have you ever been having a good day; Until someone ticked you off;
Then after you calmed down; Wondered what you got so mad about?

Have you ever had dreams; That you felt were shattered;
No longer working towards them; Because you felt it didn't matter?

Have you ever been told you are a nobody; And you begin to believe the words they said;
To the point; It started messing with your head?

Have you ever given someone or something your all; And the outcome wasn't what you liked;
So you put your head down; And just gave up on the fight?

Have you ever failed at something; And figured you couldn't succeed;
So you gave up and walked away; As if you no longer believed?

Have you ever had faith; The size of a mustardseed?
Because if you do; Please continue to believe.

That GOD has a plan and purpose; For your life that is so clever;
So I ask you again; Have you ever?

Listen Up!

And hear the voices –
That gives you the opportunity –
To make choices.

Listen up!
To your mother and father –
Your grandparents as well –
For they have great stories to tell.

Listen up!
To your teachers –
Get that education –
Make a better life for yourself –
Never lose your motivation.

Listen up!
And hear the words –
Or listen to the sound –
Of the chirping birds.

Listen up!
To the things you need to hear –
To help you in life –
So you have no fear.

Listen up!
Pay attention to what's around –
You'll be surprised –
At what can be found.

        Listen up!

Choices

In life we have choices
That we make
Like some people love
And other people hate

Be conscientious of your decisions
In all that you do
Because the malicious or deceitful ones
Has a tendency to boomerang on you

Don't allow people
To control your actions
Because they only play a small part
In a larger mathematical fraction

Be true to yourself
By keeping it real
Don't change for people
Change because of how you feel

Everyone won't like you
But who cares
Life is a big ball of experiences
That's going to take you some of everywhere

When its all said and done
And you remember all the voices
You'll sit back and be proud
That in life you made your own choices

Reflections

Look in the mirror
Who do you see
Is the person starring back
Really me?

Standing and starring
What do you do
Make faces and the person
Makes faces at you?

Thinking back
When you were young
Laughing at yourself
Remembering the fun

Going way back
Sometimes not far enough
Remembering loved ones lost
And how you had to be tough

To get through the sorrow
To make it to tomorrow
With a smile on your face
To see another day

Thinking about people you've met
Over the years
Some you've lost contact with
Others you still share laughs and tears

Life sure has brought
Some characters your way
And you're glad you have them
On any given day

Through the ups and the downs
Your smiles and frowns
Luckily life brought you certain people
You enjoy being around

You're surrounded by a wonderful circle
Who cares and shows their affection
So continue to stay true to thee
Which is the beautiful reflection

Excuse Me Ms. / Pardon Me Mr.

YOU SAID YOU LOVE ME,
SAID YOU CARED,
BUT YOU ALLOWED HIM TO BEAT ME,
NOW I'M SCARED.

      YOU WANT ME TO TRUST YOU,
      BELIEVE WHAT YOU SAY,
      BUT YOU NEGLECT ME,
      ALMOST EVERYDAY.

            WHEN I TELL YOU I'M HUNGRY,
            PLEASE FIX ME SOMETHING TO EAT,
            YOU REFUSE ME WITH NO PROBLEM,
            TELL ME TO GO TAKE A SEAT.

I TOLD YOU I HAVE HOMEWORK,
AND I NEED YOUR HELP,
YOU LOOK AT ME – TURN – AND WALK AWAY,
I'M LEFT STANDING BY MYSELF.

      WHY DO YOU TREAT ME THIS WAY?
      WHAT DID I DO?
      TO LOSE THE LOVE,
      I DESERVE FROM YOU?

            WHY DO YOU TREAT ME SO MEAN?
            YOU HAVE SUCH A COLD HEART,
            WE LIVE IN THE SAME HOUSE,
            BUT IT'S LIKE WE LIVE SO FAR APART.

HE GOT MAD AT ME!
PICKED UP A BELT,
NOW MY ENTIRE BODY,
IS FULL OF WHEPS.

                YOU DIDN'T STOP HIM!
                 YOU LET IT GO ON!
            YOU COMPLETELY INGNORED IT,
              NOW MY SPIRIT IS TORN.

                              WHY DO YOU DO ME LIKE THIS?
                                  LISTEN, MOMMY – LISTEN,
                                  PLEASE DON'T WALK AWAY!
                            EXCUSE ME MS. / PARDON ME MR.

Tick-Tock

They dropped out of high school,
Starting hanging on the streets,
Getting arrested,
By the same cops on the beat.

Parents going to the station,
Trying to figure out what's going on,
Waiting for some answers,
So their kids can come home.

Kids get released,
Having no consideration,
Right back on the streets,
Without any hesitation.

Giving their parents a hard time,
Not wanting to listen,
Just out for themselves,
On a personal mission.

Family has talked to them,
Telling them to get it together,
But they only want to hang out,
No matter what the weather.

Attempts at education,
Worked for some, but not for all,
So they headed back to the streets,
Winter / Spring / Summer / Fall.

Before they realized,
Years had passed them by,
Still doing the same'ole thing,
At the age of Twenty-Five.

Time waits for no one,
The hands on the clock – Still hanging on the block
The silence, then the sound,
Of the Tick and the Tock.

Don't Block Your Blessings

Oh my LORD; I'm starting to understand your word;
The things you have said; Is starting to stick in my head.

I've been wondering; Why my luck isn't so good;
So I sat back and reflected; Over my life, if you would.

I begin to notice things; About my past;
It was like watching pictures; They continued to flash.

I saw where and how I used to be; To where and who I am now;
Funny thing is; There's not been much change somehow.

I realized; I've been trying to make it all on my own;
Not paying much attention; To the signs I've been shown.

Been living my life; An eye for an eye;
Not caring about things or other people feelings; Sometimes not even mine.

Always thought; Things were all about me;
Not understanding; But now I see.

Now I know that the world; Does not revolve around me or anyone else;
We live on this earth; And are given many tests.

Whether we pass or fail; It's up to me and you;
But we cannot act like we are the creator of the
    Universe; Because it's not ours to do.
I finally realized; Life is all about lessons;

**Be careful how you treat others;
Because you don't know if you are blocking your blessings.**

A Love Lost

You met – fell in love – got married
New house – new car – Perfect loving family

The kids are born – you're still in school
Husband at work – everything is cool

Come home from class – have dinner on the table
Husband home from a long days work – kids talking about school
Life is very stable

The months & years fly by – almost got your degree
Start noticing changes in the husband – wondering what it could be

He started out this nice loving man – who flipped
    the script and became bitter and mean
The once happy family – now seemed to be a lost dream

Can't get the husband to communicate – kids wondering what's wrong
The hostility in the air – of a house that once was home

You've prayed about your marriage – you really tried to work it out
But things just seemed to get worse – you begin
    having more and more doubt

Now the husband decides to leave – just doesn't
    want to be with you anymore
Your family has fallen apart – you stand there looking at a closed door

You were a good wife – and a good mother
But he found love – in the arms of another

Your heart hurts – your body full of aches and pain
Because of a love that once was – of what seemed to be the perfect man

As time goes on – you heart heals
You move on with your life – over the years

Sometimes looking back – and measuring the cost
Of a love that once was – that became a love lost

Life In The Fast Lane

14 years old,
Out in the streets,
Selling her body,
Like a cheap piece of meat.

Parents don't want anything to do with her,
Family has turned their backs,
Got no where to go,
They've deemed her a filthy tramp.

She used to be a straight A student,
Went on to High School,
Got caught up with the wrong crowd,
Caught up with the wrong dude.

Started having her turn tricks,
First 3 times a week, then everyday,
Parents noticed some changes,
Some modifications in her ways.

She was scared to tell the truth,
So she told many lies,
Parents so caught up in their own lives,
Didn't notice the horror in her eyes.

Parents eventually found out,
What their little girl was doing,
They got so disgusted,
Told her she was ruined.

Never once did they attempt to help her,
Or try to understand,
Their 14-year-old girl,
Was being controlled by a grown man.

Now at Twenty-Two,
She's still in the game,
Got girls working under her,
Living life in the fast lane.

Neighborhood Drug Dealer

Come on! Come on!
Got that dime bag;
Open it up;
Puff-Puff, Pass.

Got that Barney & Powder too;
I'm the moneymaker;
And I'm looking for you.

I don't care about your age;
I don't discriminate;
Give me my money;
I don't negotiate.

I got that good stuff;
Keep you higher than high;
If you got the money;
You got the buy.

I'm on the block everyday;
You know I'm trying to get paid;
If you need something – you let me know;
I know exactly where to go.

Damn, here come the cops;
Let me stash my goodies;
Oh hell! I'm cool;
That's just those two rookies.

It's so many drug dealers out here;
Standing on every block;
But I'll sell you that good stuff;
I even sell rocks.

You just let me know what you want;
I waste no time;
I'll get it to you so fast;
It'll blow your mind.

Who's my supplier;
Is the question you ask;
Well, if I keep it real or even realer;
Truth be told, anyone's mother, father, sister or
    brother can be the neighborhood Drug Dealer.

Haters

Are people who want what you have
They want what you got
But don't have a pot to piss in
Or a window to throw it out

They are irritated
Seemingly discombobulated
And will smile in your face
But want to take your place

They talk about you behind your back
Such a cowardly act
Wishing they could be behind the wheel of your automobile
Your identity they'd quickly steal

Sometimes they cringe at your presence
Highly upset about your motivation
Say all kinds of negative things about you
And the oxymoron is that they would love to do what you do

They comment on everything
From your hair to your clothes, your car to your house
They become so fixated on you
They don't know how to shut their mouth

Always talking trash
Like a loud mouth in class
So worried about you
Things in their lives start to slip through

You have to watch a Hater
Pay close attention
Like watching a T.V. show
Before the intermission

They can be slick
They can be bold
Plots and plans to bring you down
Their hearts are very cold

Hateration is real
Not false, but true
You never know if you got a Hater
Who is in your Crew

So keep an eye out and your ears open
For some things that may come to light
Don't be surprised if you ever discover
A Hater to your left and to your right

Sometimes they are the ones you never thought
Would act in such a way
And always remember
A Hater dreams to live life in your shoes everyday!

The Man at the Entrance

There was a man who stood alone
I overheard him talking in a very soft tone

I took a glance to see his face
Surprisingly it was full of dignity and grace

He didn't say much as we waited to get in
He was with no one, he had no friends

I felt sorry for him, because I could see through his pain
I wondered how he could sustain

He was dressed not tacky, but decent enough
He looked okay, he didn't look rough

Many people walked pass and didn't speak
Just starring at this man with a small physic

As we waited to get into the movie theater while standing in line
I heard him ask someone if they had a dime

The woman looked at him and snubbed her nose
Thinking he was some old homeless man begging, I suppose

I walked over to him and gave him 10 cents
He looked at me and said "Thank you Miss"

"You are the first person who has taken the time
To walk over to me with compassion in mind"

I told him that there was something about him that I could not place
He had such a familiar face

We conversated for a short while as we waited
I kept thinking to myself, there is something about this man that is so elated

We finally got in to see the movie "Passion of The Christ"
I looked for the man, to my left and to my right

I didn't see him, he was no where to be found
The wind blew and I saw some paper on the ground

I picked it up as it blew right to my feet
And what I read, I had to take a seat

It read "Thank you for your time, talking with me while you waited and even giving me 10 cents. You are a true child of GOD, it's written all over you and in all that you do. Continue to be the person you are and I know we will meet again someday. I was at the movie theater to see the people who came out to see my story, and the reactions of those who had already saw."

I was puzzled, was this some crazy person I just talked to?
Did he think he was Christ?

I went on to watch the movie
The agony and the pain
That our LORD endured
So that we could live again

As I was leaving the show
I saw the same man
Standing in line again

I walked over to him
Showed him the note
He looked at me and smiled
And said "now you know"

I replied "know what, I don't understand"
Then what I saw
I could no longer stand

I saw the holes in his hand
A light surrounded this man
He said to me "there's one thing I didn't mention
We will meet again one day and I'll be the Man at the Entrance."

Be good, Do good, Live good – We never know who we will meet along our journey, but we do know who is keeping a journal.

Life is too Short

Live life to the fullest each and everyday, you never know when your time is up. Don't live life by other people's standards. Live life by your standards, be happy, be loving, be kind. People will try to make you believe that you are suppose to do for them, live your life according to them, make your world revolve around them. GOD made us each individuals for a purpose. Stress is best when Free is added to the end. So…

Don't harbor hatred, it only tears down your soul

Don't hold grudges, it only eats you up whole

Smile, GOD has given you another day

Laugh, no matter what people say

Do good, it makes you feel a world apart

Love others, it's good for your heart

Live, Laugh and Love – Life is too short not to

Life is like a deck of cards

You don't deal with the hand that you were dealt, its all in how you Play with the hand you were dealt. Optimal words "Deal" and "Play". If you deal with it, you may never win, never overcome, never achieve higher levels. But if you play, you will lose some, you will win some, therefore you become a Player of life and not live a life whereby you are Played.

*Written By,
Yolanda Jackson*

Summertime

The weather is nice
The breeze feels good
School is out & the office is closed
Chillin in the hood as you normally would

Got your best clothes on
Brand new shoes
Car shined up
Every body is starring at you

You see your boys
They jump in the whip
Driving down
The Lake Shore Drive strip

Pull up to the beach
Meet up with some friends
Sitting back just chillin
Checking out the trends

Got my girls with me
We looking fly
Not trying to hook up with anyone
But we are checking out prospects as they walk by

The sun is shining
It's nice and hot
Just hanging out
Is what it's about

No drama
No drugs
No worries
No thugs

It's a nice day out
Living life and having fun
Blue skies
Bright yellow sun

If all days were like today
I surely wouldn't mind
Having it like this 24-7
The joys and fun of summertime

Little Brother

Let me whisper in your ear
Help you to understand
The reason we need you
To grow up to be a good man

The world has already tainted you
Tries to make people believe you have no worth
But you were crowned a King
At the beginning of your birth

Don't let the hypocrites
The society as whole
Tear you down
And break your soul

You are a powerhouse
A force to be reckoned with
You have the ability
To create your own niche

Make sure you raise your children
Be an excellent role model
Don't let the world believe
You are dead-beat fathers

You don't have to be
A product of your environment
Make a real life for your family
So you all can enjoy your retirement

Invest your money
Build a future
Learn about stocks
Don't be afraid, let it allure you

Get that education
Don't hang out on the block
Transform your knowledge
Into a solid building rock

Don't be abusive
Don't degrade your women
God made you in his image
In the very beginning

Little brother, you are bad
A magnificent piece of art
Stop living by your head
And start living by your heart

I love ya!

Little Sister

You are beautiful
You are smart
Don't continue to think
You are just some body parts

When GOD created you
For sure we know
That within you
Our population continues to grow

We are mothers, sisters, aunts
Nieces, grandmothers and friends
We feed off of each other
From beginning to end

Don't allow anyone to break you down
You are strong, powerful women
Who wear a mighty crown

You deserve the best that life has to offer
Don't believe your only worth
Is lying on your back
And being treated like dirt

Carry yourselves with class
By the way you talk and the way you dress
Keep your mind focused
And others will be impressed

But don't live for others
You must live for you
Be proud of yourself
And all that you do

You don't understand
The power that you have
From where our sisters before us came
And looking at our successful sisters now

Little sister you are a fabulous
You are nothing less than a Queen
Don't you let anyone
Strip you of your self-being

I love ya!

God is in my head

God is my head
Every single day
Each morning I wake up
To him I pray

Every night before I fall asleep
I pray to the father above
For blessing me and all my family
And for his undying love

I think of him
And all his goodness
His Grace and his Mercy
That has brought me through

God is in my head
Twenty-Four Seven
I do my best
Because I want to go to Heaven

Don't get me wrong
I have done and still sometimes do dirt
And I've apologized
For anyone I ever hurt

I live my life
To please only one man
For he is the one I will see
On Judgment Day, and stand

Before him in all my goodness
And in all my bad too
Knowing that he has forgave and forgiven
My sins through and through

I gave my life to him
At the age of 20
I have a spiritual connection
That is good and plenty

I LOVE GOD
Yeah God is in my head
He wakes me, feeds me
Comforts my days

God is in my head
I am so thankful for that
He's brought me a mighty long ways
And I'm not looking back

I continue to grow in him
Everyday of my life
Thank you Father GOD
For making my wrongs into a right

God is in my head
I hope he's in yours too
Live life more abundantly
For that is what he wanted for you

#1 Consumer

My brothers and sisters
Listen to this
We spend our money
And this is not a myth
We contribute to this society
We contribute to this world
It is our money
That can make a head twirl
Estimated 200 (+) billion dollars spent last year
And 330 (+) billion spent the year before
Spending money in this world
Like never before
We keep the economy going
We keep the money stacked high
We keep big wigs pockets filled
But what about you
How much money do you make?
How much do you let the economy take?
How much money do you spend?
Until you've reached the very end
And we continue to do so
Day after day, week after week
Realize our power, it is not bleek
We purchase an assortment of valuables
Spending money on so many things
Styling and profiling
While continuously buying
Making this world rich
Ain't that a bitch!
Then you can't get a loan
To buy you a home

I'm not talking about those who have jacked up their credit
I'm talking about the ones who have the money to make it
But discrimination and predatory lending
Attempts to stop you from spending
Or building
For what every hard-working person is striving for
A house, a home, just having your own
Being sought out on job applications
Codes based upon the races
Not getting hired because of the color of your skin
When will this madness end!
But you can continue to buy the products the company makes
Keeping them rich, while they want to hate?
Realize the power of your pocket
Of your wallet
We are not the majority?
Now that is some bull
We are the ones with the true pull
Try not buying one single thing
In any given day
Watch how the economy
Crashes is such a nasty way
We can make it or break it in 24 hours
Can I say this any LOUDER!
So to hell with what people say
About my race of people
How about that for humor?
Recognize, we are the #1 Consumer

My Mind Struggles

My mind struggles – to understand
Why people keep killing
It gives me a numb feeling.

My mind struggles – to figure out why
Some people
Make their parents cry.

My mind struggles – to figure out
What this chaos
Is all about.

My mind struggles – and asks the question
Why do we hurt each other
Without hesitation.

My mind struggles – and I wonder
Why is there so much evil
In this world before us.

My mind struggles – to make sense
Of this craziness
Of this madness.

*My mind struggles – and I think back
Of how our ancestors and past leaders
Fought for the Civil Rights Act.*

*My mind struggles – and the thoughts can't fade
Why so many people don't realize
The sacrifices that were made.*

*My mind struggles – and has its own fight
Trying to understand
Why people won't get right?*

*My mind struggles – and it asks
Why so many people are not moving forward
But taking thousands of steps backwards?*

*My mind struggles – as I write this poetic letter
Begging people to please get it together
And become better.*

My mind struggles.

Hip-hop Memory Lane

RUN DMC – King of Rock & Walk this way
Adidas with fat or no shoestrings
Do you remember those days?

Queen Latifah - Ladies first
Up in the club
Screaming til it felt like your lungs would burst

Kurtis Blow – Basketball
Made the sport a song
Singing it in the school halls

MC Lyte - Georgie Porgie Puddin Pie & I am the Lyte
Dancing like crazy
Hands waving to the sky

Sugarhill Gang – Don't push me cause I'm close to the edge
Still singing that song
In my head

Roxanne Shante – Roxanne Roxanne I wanna be your man
Bumping the sounds
In the 6 door van

Kool Moe Dee – Wild Wild West
Put leather clothes
To the test

LL Cool J – I'm bad
Kango hat
Began a new fad

Lisa Lisa & Cult Jam – Wonder if I take you home
Had some bad music
It was a hot song

Rob Base – I wanna rock right now
If this didn't get you up on your feet
I don't understand how

Salt-N-Peppa & Spinderella – Push It
Had you doing back-bends
To no end

MC Breed – Ain't No Future in Yo Frontin'
We had this song bumpin'
While we were stuntin'

Whoodini – Friends
How many of us have them?
This question never ends

Rockmaster Scott & The Dynamic Three – The Roof is on fire
At the party our hands went higher
Cause we didn't give a ____ let the mutha___ burn
This was one of the best songs

Frankie Smith – Double Dutch Bus
Coming down the street
Now this song made you get up out your seat

These songs were HOT
And there were so many more
Dancing and jamming
Until your feet and body were sore

Snapping your fingers
Nodding your head
Feeling the beat
Repeating all lyrics that were said

(continues)

Beastie Boys – Brass Monkey
And Paul Revere
Hip-Hop old school
Was very fierce

New School Hip-Hop
Is also on and slammin
Tupac, Biggie, NAS, Jay Z, Kanye, Common just to name a few
These brotha's be jamming

Hip-Hop old
Hip-Hop new
They continue to have us
Move and groove

Hip-Hop continues to grow
Hip-Hop continues to change
So I hope you enjoyed this brief trip
Down Hip-Hop memory lane!

The Sky Is The Limit

- Dreams and Motivation

Determination and Pursuit of Happiness

- Do what you do to get where you need to get

Never allow anyone to deter you

- Don't feed into negativity

There is a positive in every negative situation

- As the song goes "Tell Your Storm"

That it won't last long

- Don't give up

Keep fighting for what you believe in

- Remember "The race is not won by the swift nor the strong, but to the one who endureth until the end"

In order to get something, you have to fight for it

- Be humble in your journey

It will earn you overwhelming strength

- Pray the entire duration

You need a good friend to see you through the difficult times

- Keep your head high as you reach for the stars

The only obstacles you cannot overcome are the ones you've determined you cannot hurdle over – MIND OVER MATTER

- Be strong, be bold, take charge of your situation

The Sky is the Limit and you are a winner

What I Do

I do my best to please the crowd,
While writing and rhyming,
All about timing,
Writing deep thoughts,
Giving people something to think & talk about,
Keeping it real all the time,
Being original with mine,
Making the world rethink many things,
Just reaching out to all human beings,
My flow is smooth,
You can keep up with the groove,
Some say my flow is tight,
They love the way I write,
I try and capture the essence of life,
Things we live and see day and night,
Thoughts come to my head and with a thought I run,
Sometimes writing until my hand is numb,
But it's all good - because I get great feedback,
And I like that,
You keep me going,
You keep me flowing,
Life keeps me focused and grounded,

So I can write all about it,
I'll keep writing,
Because I'm liking,
The way this is moving,
The way my words are grooving,
The people who continue to read,
And like what they see,
The people – the crowd,
The noise is getting loud,
I'm feeling what you are saying,
You enjoy my realness, there is no playing,
So I continue to write for me,
And be the best I can be,
I continue to write for you,
Cause this is what I do.

I dedicate this poem to ALL my readers (past, present and future) I Love Ya!

Back In The Day

Do you remember when we were young
Outside playing
Having a ball
No cell phones and no pagers

Mom said be in front of the house
Before the street lights were on
You made sure you were
Otherwise she would wear out your buns

Mom and dad raised you
But the neighbors did too
There was no talking back
Trying to show off in front of your Crew

Curfew was implemented
Education taking seriously
Teachers made phone calls to your home
It scared you immensely

You had to ask if you could go out
And you made sure you stayed where you were told
There were no sudden movements
You just were not that bold

Televisions were black and white
Some of us had color
There were no remote controls
You used your little sisters or brothers

The words "thank you" were words you spoke
There was a level of respect
If you didn't give it
Mom and dad were capable of "ringing your neck"

When the fight jumped off
The crowd gathered around
No gunshots ringing out
Just folks rolling around on the ground

The school parties were a big event
Got your party clothes out the week before
Talked about it Monday – Friday
And when Friday came you got geeked up even more

No Computers
Or reality TV
But there were after school specials
That you couldn't wait to see

Best time to get what you wanted
Was when mom was on the phone
She told you yes
So you would just leave her alone

But if you tried to be slick
It definitely caught up
Because after she was off the phone and realized
You got put on punishment or had a very sore butt

When you had birthday parties
It was a neighborhood invite
And one of the best gifts you got
Was that banana seat bike

We used ice-cream sticks
To put in our bicycle wheels
Made it sound like a motorcycle
Those were our thrills

(continues)

Skates use to have metal wheels
You strapped up to your shoes
There was not much fancy footwork
More like very simple moves

When it was hot
You made kool aid and put it in the freezer
With the plastic Popsicle maker
Mixing cherry, strawberry, grape – all the flavors

Candy was really a penny
Phone calls were really a dime
Cigarettes were really 80 cents
And the words "no cobbs" was used all the time

Phil Collins "Air Tonight"
Colonel Abrams "I'm Trapped"
Michael Jackson "PYT"
Were some of the songs we talked about

Yeah I remember those times
Wasn't that long ago
Now things are a totally different way
But it was good times, back in the day

This poem is for all of us mid 60's & 70's babies - just a rhymes to remind us how much fun we had back in the day and how times have changed overall in such a short period of time.

Daily Prayer

Father God head of my life
Help me today to get it right
Let me not hold on to yesterdays madness
But latch on to today's gladness
Make me a better person by every second, minute and hour
Help me bloom today like a beautiful flower
May I remember who is in control
Who has the floor
Who has helped me walk through a new door
Let me not beat up on myself
Or be so frustrated with another
That it changes my attitude
Towards my sisters and my brothers
Thank you God for waking me this day
And starting me on my way
Let me not get weary by what others say
But help me to continue to pray
I ask that you make me strong when I seem weak
Help me to maintain a powerful physic
Let not my appearance seem overbearing but humble / meek
And give me the proper words to speak
Help me this day and those to follow
To understand I should never wallow
For you are my strength day and night
You provide me with an awesome might
So Father God I ask you again
To walk with me as my day begins
Stand by my side through it all
Making sure I will not fall
Help me pick the right words
When I open my mouth
Let the beauty of your love
Flow right on out
Word after word, layer after layer
This Father God is my daily prayer

The Cries of the Street

You turn on the news;
What do you see?
The death of yet another;
Human Being.

So many are young;
Young adults and small children;
What is really going on?
This is a state of confusion!

Our kids can't enjoy a nice day;
Because gun shots keep ringing out;
Killing our youth;
What is that about?

People scared to leave their homes;
Scared to go to work;
Don't know if someone;
Is lurking and ready to hurt.

School kids are dying;
Getting killed by the dozens;
Gangs are running rampant;
Killing our loved ones one after another.

Young men and women;
Are being shot and killed;
While minding their own business;
Someone tell me this isn't real!

My 22-year-old brother lost his life;
From the hands of another;
Now my family mourns;
In this time of trouble.

How do we fight this war?
Right at our front door;
So much genocide;
Right before our eyes.

So many lost;
This is too deep;
Can you hear;
The cries of the street?

Many paid the price

Look to your left
Look to your right
Someone you're looking at
Has paid the price

Either personally
Or through past generations
Yet still today, we have
Hurts and frustrations

Pioneers of the land
The Marches that went forth
For so many people
To be able to freely walk the earth

Young people pick up a book
Earn some knowledge
Get off the street corners
And into classrooms of a University or College

Pay it forward
Give it back
Education is key
Its not whack

Learn your heritage
From where you come
Know that this is
God's home

Past struggles
Present issues
Hold your head high
Keep working toward your vision

There is something I don't understand
Through every thing in the past
Why do our young brother's
Kill one another
How can you look into the eyes
Of another human being
Pull the trigger
How can you be so mean?

Our people along with other races
Fought for our rights
To be able to live a fair life
I can't fathom the reasoning of this strife

So many killings
Day after day
Brother killing brother
This just isn't the way

Too many people have died
And sometimes it seems in vain
Because what we see on the news everyday or experience in life
Is completely insane!

Can someone explain to me
The mindset of our youth
I'm perplexed
So I'm looking for the truth

(continues)

Why is there genocide?
So many homicides
And there is no hesitation
About the lives being taken

It angers my heart
It angers my soul
That people can so easily kill
That people are so bold

People listen to me
When I tell you
The Civil Rights Movement
Was to see us through

To get us to a better place
Although discrimination and racism still exists
It is very prevalent
With the Jena 6

Gang violence has taken the life
Of an innocent 10-year old boy
My prayers go out to the family
Of little Arthur Jones

Gun shots ring out
Now 14-year old Samuel is dead
Gun man came back in anger over a bike
And shot this young man in the head!

I lost my own brother this year
Because of senseless gun violence
And it's getting worse too
R.I.P. little bro, we love you Cinque

U.S. Troops fighting a War
Overseas in Iraq
Make no mistake about it
Many have paid the price

IT IS TIME to walk through the door
Of a brand new light
We are a powerful people
When we stand together and fight

Not fight as in violence
But to have regard for human life
Never forgetting
Many paid the price

Eyes to the Soul

Grandma said
People's eyes are the key to their soul
There are stories to be told

Eyes can tell you a story of pain
A story of joy
A story of sorrow

Eyes can tell you lies
Or the truth
Eyes of the old and of the youth

Eyes can tell you a story of love
A story of mystery
Even a story of history

Eyes can tell you myths
Stories from the abyss
Even stories of bliss

Eyes can tell you a story of happiness
A story of stories
Eyes can tell you about worries

Look into someone's eyes when you talk
You can read what they are all about
You'll walk away with no doubts

A person's mouth can tell you a lie
Their actions can be of deceit
But their eyes, they cannot defeat

Eyes are key
Because they will unfold
The very essence of your soul

Visions Of The Senses

Close your eyes – Grab hold of a thought
Construct it – Make it a masterpiece of Art

Open your mouth – Verbalize the pieces
Taste the structure – Like the Mona Lisa

Smell the scents – All colors of paint
Put it all together – Like putting money in the bank

Listen to the form – Hear the work being done
Imagine joy – Like a child having fun

Touch the art – And collaborate all that has been mentioned
Now uncover to the world – Your visions of the senses

Stars

Have you ever went out at night
Looked up at the sky
Saw the darkness
But also saw it as bright

Looking up into the universe
Wondering what's out there
Trying to figure out
While you're engrossed in a long stare

No birds are flying in the air
The crickets making a loud noise
The noises of the night
Feeling just right

The sun has set
The moon has rose
The breeze is cooler
An Eagle soars

The rush of the day is gone
The settling of the night begins
You sit on the porch
While chatting with family and friends

You look up to the sky
To find a piece of mind
It opens up for you
As it does all the time

It reaches to no end
The sky is the limit
You can get lost
Starring with imagination

The moon is bright
It lights the earth
It's like night
Is a brand new birth

With lights all around & inspiration in the air
Like a no-hold-bars
The night encourages us
To continue to reach for the Stars

The Stain of Pain

Life is too short
This we know
Never knowing
When it's our time to go

I woke up one morning (5/8/07)
Went on to work
Got a phone call
That could have given someone a stroke

My mother on the other line
Telling me my 22 year old brother was shot
This is just something
I would have never thought about

I left work
Got on the bus
Prayed to God
Didn't make a fuss

Two stops before I got to my car
A few short blocks until I got in my ride
Another phone call from mom
"Cinque has died"

My face is stunned
My heart confused
Not understanding
Why this happened to you

I called the family
Called some friends
Informing them
My brother's life had come to an end

Still frozen in time
My mind working overload
Just saw my brother
A few days ago

We were talking about GOD
Talking about Life
Talking about the future
Man, this can't be right

Someone took his life
They had no regard
Could care less
About our stress

As he stood and talked with friends
Laughing and talking smack
The gunman
Shot my brother in the back

He fled the scene
Still at large
I pray everyday
Knowing he has to answer to GOD

Now we've lost our brother
Mom and Dad, their son
His five children, their father
His life gone at the hand of a gun

Someone pulled the trigger
Never did they figure
The ripple effect it would have
Senseless Crime, its so sad

(continues)

I thank God
For the 22 years
He gave me with my brother
Although I still shed tears

We conversated a lot
We had a real connection
I now think of Q as my guardian angel
My protection

I love you Q
Just the same
We'll see you again, but until then
We live with the stain of pain

My brother lived his life knowing Christ died for our sins and he lived his life by giving love, which is why I know, he's with the Father Above.

A Paradise

The wind in your hair
Sand on your feet
The serene sounds of water
On a beautiful white beach

Palm trees swaying
Kids are playing
Birds are flying
No one is crying

You are at peace
With your surroundings
A quiet place
No sad faces

There is no war
No fighting going on
People are kind
And full of love

The skies are blue
Picture perfect place
No chaos
No place for hate

(continues)

The streets are gold
The gates are white
The music is playing
The tunes just right

You see family
You see friends
And this time around
There is no end

Everyone wears a smile
That extends from ear to ear
All eyes are dry
No more shedding tears

No more violence or chaos
You are with God and Christ
Do right in this life
And you will arrive at this Paradise

Weekday Journey

I sit
I listen
People Talking
People Walking

Good Morning
Good Evening
Excuse Me Ms.
Excuse Me Mr.

Hey how are you doing
How was your day
Same ole same
Nothing to really say

Phone rings
Talking begins
Some loud
Some whisper in the wind

See a co-worker
See a friend
The ride home
Quickly ends

Another Day
Another dollar
Is sometimes what I hear
People holla

Boss man was trippin
Boss lady keeps knit-picking
They getting on my nerves
But gotta go back I suppose

(continues)

Make that money
To pay the bills
Working hard
No big thrills

See ya tomorrow
They holla as they rise
Another walks by they know
To their surprise
Almost at the end
Of the line
Get up to give the seat
To the blind

Traffic is a mess
Seems like forever
To get to your stop
Start getting your things together

Now you are next
Your daily commutes ends
But starts over again
The next morning

You say see ya later
Have a nice night
Head on home
With great delight

Some days are hilarious
Some just funny
But there's always something to talk about
On my weekday journey

Ego Trippin

Some people always thinking –
They know what they are talking about –
Always trying to show you –
Always trying to show out.

They think they have it figured –
Their head getting bigger –
Can't tell them they are wrong –
They can't take it, they aren't that strong.

Trying to put you on the spot –
Whenever they have the chance –
Trying to make their point –
Trying to make their stand.

Half the time they are wrong –
But will swear they are right –
You can't get a word in edgewise –
Because they'll put up a fight.

You find these people everywhere –
In church, on the job, even family –
Always trying to be smart about something –
Thinking they are so handy.

You can't tell them nothing –
They know it all –
Will argue with you forever –
Their mouth won't stall!

(continues)

They figure they got it going on –
They build themselves up so high –
Looking down on everyone around –
Thinking they are so fly.

Bottom line is –
They aren't that smart –
Just trying to be someone –
Who they truly are not.

But they irritate you to no end –
Like a bug bite that keeps itching –
So full of themselves –
But are only ego trippin!

FYI

I love you

I swear I do

I just wish you felt

The same way too

You are in my dreams

I fantasize of looking in your eyes

The beauty of your soul

Is what my mind holds

Your lips so soft

Your heart so kind

I just wish

You were mine

You walk pass

And catch my eye

Your sexiness

Gives me a high

You keep me on edge

With every breath you take

Your figure/build so beautiful

The sculpture of your face

Your walk

Your talk

Your sex appeal

Is the real deal

I caress you softly

(continues)

Your every being
You make me melt
Inside and out
Your entire persona
Is what I love about
You
Who gives me chills
As well as thrills
On my mind
All the time
I want to hold you
Mold you
Be with you
In all I do
Then I awake
And begin
To realize
My dream has come to an end
So I smile
And say "alright"
Waiting for darkness to fall
Can't wait to be with you again tonight

How I feel about you

You keep me laughing
Keep a smile on my face
You have great conversation
Day after day
You teach me about things
You help me fulfill my dreams
You are my listening ear
What I say, you always hear
If I need a shoulder to lean on
You give me yours
Without hesitation
You have great consideration
Your eyes give me hope
Your words give me faith
You are a generous giver
Hardly ever do you take
We can talk to the wee hours of the morning
Or late at night
You correct me when I'm wrong
And applaud me when I'm right
I look to you for guidance
When I'm lost and need direction
You keep me focused
Helping me with my meditation
Your silliness can break the ice
Of a long standing silence
Your sincerity is always appreciated
Because you keep it real on all levels
Yet your sense of humor
Can fill laughter in a room
Like a funny cartoon
Your smile can brighten someone's day
Because it is warm and inviting

(continues)

Your personality is calm
You are cool and collective
Always being selective
With the words you say and how you treat others
Which is why I love so many things about you
You've taught me so many things
How to be a better human being
Your very essence is so clever
You are like a cool breeze…the weather
You've always been true
This is how I feel about you

Your Season

Day by Day
Month by Month
Year by Year
Believe it
It will come
Have no fear

Doors are opening
Things will happen
Blessings are on the way
Keep the Faith
Hold your head high
Trust in his word & continue to pray

Don't be depressed
Look ahead
Feel the Joy
You'll go through situations
It has to happen
In order to give you more

God has to move things around
Removing things & people
In order to put you in a position
To gain
To maintain
To grow in your mission

Love God
Through the good & the bad
You go through circumstances for a reason
But hold steadfast
Never losing Faith
For you are about to enter your season

Printed in the United States
113850LV00003B/355-372/P